THE ESSENTIAL FOUCAULT

THE ESSENTIAL FOUCAULT

Paul Strathern

BOOKS

This edition published in Great Britain in 2002 by
Virgin Books Ltd
Thames Wharf Studios
Rainville Road
London
W6 9HA

First published in the USA in 2000 as *Foucault in 90 Minutes* by Ivan R Dee

A catalogue record for this book is available from the British Library.

ISBN 0 7535 0684 X

CONTENTS

INTRODUCTION

Foucault was not a philosopher in the classical tradition. Even so, at one stage in his life he was regarded in some quarters as the new Kant – an absurdly overblown estimation. But this was hardly Foucault's fault (even if he did little to discourage such opinions). It was also hardly his fault that the very possibility of being a classical philosopher was completely beyond him. This is no mere intellectual judgement. The fact is, Wittgenstein had to all intents and purposes brought philosophy in the classical tradition to a close. Wittgenstein had insisted there was no longer any such thing as philosophy – just philosophising. Most major philosophical questions were the result of linguistic errors. Untangle the mistake, and the question simply disappeared. And any remaining questions were simply unanswerable (or, more correctly, unaskable).

But a variant of the classical philosophical tradition did persist in continental Europe, in the work of Heidegger. This claimed to operate beyond Wittgensteinian realms, beyond the reach of logic, analysing the very grounds of our thought and apprehension. Foucault was heavily influenced by this tradition. It led him to uncover how philosophy, and indeed all 'knowledges', arrive at their versions of the truth. He showed that such 'truths' depended largely upon the assumptions, or mind-set, or the age in which they were promulgated.

Foucault set about his task like a historian rather than a philosopher. Painstakingly he researched original documents from the period he was investigating. These revealed first-hand the society, knowledge, and power structure of the age in question. Foucault concluded that knowledge and power were so closely related that he collated them in his term 'power/knowledge'. This was the central issue of his philosophy. But in reaching it, and investigating its implications, he covered a wide range of often sensational material. Madness, sexuality, discipline and punishment – the history of such topics was considered essential to his argument. Add to this the relation of these topics to his personal life, and you have the most sensational philosopher of modern times.

Yet how much of actual philosophical worth was contained within all this sensationalism? Nearly twenty years after his death, reactions to this question remain sharply divided. Philosophical oblivion is easily attained: the fact that Foucault is still being discussed at all is recognition of a sort. How much longer this state of affairs will continue is up to us to decide.

FOUCAULT'S LIFE AND WORKS

Paul-Michel Foucault was born on 15 October 1926, at Poitiers, 250 miles south of Paris. His family were well-to-do bourgeois in a town that has remained a byword for French provincialism. His father was a surgeon, taught at the local medical school, and ran a prosperous practice. His mother was a strong-minded woman who managed her husband's finances, helped administer his practice, and daringly drove an automobile.

Besides their town house in Poitiers, the family owned a small manor house in the country. During Paul-Michel's childhood they also built a seaside villa on the Atlantic coast at La Baule. This was large enough for a family of five and servants. Here the family spent their summer holidays amidst the pine trees overlooking a long curve of sandy beach. Father was kindly but stern, mother was efficient but concerned. For Paul-Michel, life at home with his older sister and younger brother was the epitome of normality. Such was the standard background of so many intransigent French intellectuals who have revolted against all forms of authority and bourgeois behaviour. (Although he would strive to rebel against so much else, Foucault would not be able to avoid conforming to this Gallic stereotype, which had held sway from Voltaire to Sartre.)

At school young Paul-Michel was weedy and shortsighted. As a result his schoolmates soon corrupted his name to

Polchinelle (the French equivalent of the hunchbacked figure of fun we know as Punch). Freudians will be intrigued to know that he dreamed of becoming a goldfish. Such fishy ambitions were reflected in his academic performance. Although evidently bright, he never excelled. Even at his favourite subject, history, he only finished second.

World events impinged little on sleepy Poitiers or Foucault family life. The seaside villa was built during the early years of the depression; Hitler's posturings on the newsreels were dismissed with sophisticated ridicule in the press; and the blandly debonair records of Maurice Chevalier spun on the phonograph.

When he was ten, young Paul-Michel saw the first refugees from the Spanish Civil War tramping through the streets of Poiters. Three years later Germany invaded Poland, launching World War II, and the family drove back from their summer holiday at La Baule for the last time. By the time Foucault was fourteen, the Nazis had invaded France, the French army was retreating in disarray, and even Poitiers was in turmoil. With the unbending ineptitude of an operating-theatre martinet, Dr Foucault supervised the setting up of emergency medical units in the town. In the background his wife painstakingly smoothed ruffled feathers and efficiently ensured that things got done. Now wearing glasses, but still in short pants, young Paul-Michel looked on in bewilderment. That summer his exam results plummeted.

Mother pulled strings to have him transferred to another school, whereupon the academic ugly duckling turned into a swan. This was to become something of a pattern. Foucault was to underperform at important exams but then shine when he took them a second time. At the age of twenty, on his second attempt, Foucault gained a place at the École Normale Supérieure in Paris. This was the intellectual hothouse where the *crème de la crème* of France's students were put through their paces. To be a 'normalien' marked one as a superior species for life. Normality has always been exceptional in France, and the superintellectual 'normaliens' were often a fairly odd lot. But even here Foucault soon stood out.

By now the Punch of the school playground had developed into a decidedly prickly character. During the previous year or so he had gradually become aware that he was homosexual. Such a thing was not only illegal at the time; in Poitiers it was unthinkable. Paul-Michel couldn't even turn to his beloved mother for guidance and reassurance. And by this stage he had also fallen out heavily with Papa. The adolescent Paul-Michel *refused* to follow in the family tradition and become a doctor. He just wasn't interested in medicine, and that was that. He would stamp upstairs to his room, slam the door, and bury his head in yet another volume of history. By the time he took the entrance exam to the École Normale Supérieure for the second time, there was no doubting that here was an intellectual thoroughbred. (He finished fourth in the entire country.) But there was also no doubting that he had the unpredictable temperament of a thoroughbred.

In Paris he took to calling himself plain Michel (dropping Paul, his father's name). Michel Foucault's first years at the ENS were to be a litany of incidents. On one occasion he slashed his chest with a razor; on another he had to be restrained while chasing a student with a dagger; and on another he nearly succeeded in committing suicide by taking an overdose of pills. He drank heavily and occasionally experimented with drugs (very much a minority pursuit in those far-off days). Sometimes he would disappear for nights on end, afterwards slumping back hollow-eyed and haggard into his dormitory with depression. Few guessed the truth. He was tortured with guilt over what had occurred on his lonely sexual expeditions.

Foucault was unable to live with himself, and none of the students in his dormitory wished to live with him. They looked upon him as mad and dangerous, qualities that only seemed to be exacerbated by his evident brilliance. Fiercely aggressive in intellectual argument, he was not above resorting to violence. His fellow students shunned his company, and he began developing psychosomatic illnesses. Long bouts in a solitary bed in the sanatorium spared him from the communal existence of his dormitory, and here he read voluminously, even by ENS standards.

Foucault's somewhat haphazard enthusiasm for history now found cohesion. He began reading the nineteenth-century German philosopher Hegel, whose philosophy insisted on the coherence and meaning of history. The purpose of history was its long progress towards the ultimate reality of reason and self-consciousness. According to Hegel, 'All that is rational is real, and all that is real is rational.' Below the surface of events, history had its hidden structure. 'In history we are concerned with what has been and what is; in philosophy, on the other hand, we are concerned not with what belongs exclusively to the past or even the future, but with what is, both now and eternally – that is, with reason.' History and philosophy became one, a unity that had immediate relevance to the present.

From Hegel, Foucault progressed to the twentieth-century German philosopher Heidegger, who saw the human predicament as determined by deeper elements than mere reason. 'My entire philosophical development was determined by my reading of Heidegger,' Foucault would later write. The excitement of first encountering Heidegger's thought is best conveyed by his student Hannah Arendt: 'Thinking has come to life again; the cultural treasures of the past, believed to be dead, are being made to speak, in the course of which it turns out that they propose things altogether different from the familiar worn-out trivialities they had been presumed to say.' The past was alive in the present, and how we understood the past showed how we could understand the present. History was not recording the truth of the past but revealing the truth of the present. Such was the drift of Foucault's thought.

At the time, Heidegger's philosophy was a matter of deep debate in the cafés of Left Bank Paris. Postwar disillusionment and a despair with traditional values had led to a widespread enthusiasm for the existentialism of Jean-Paul Sartre, who had himself been heavily influenced by Heidegger. Sartre's existentialism was highly subjective and believed in 'existence before essence'. There was no such thing as an essential humanity or subjectivity. This essence we ourselves created by the manner in which we existed, made our choices and acted in the world. Our subjectivity was likewise no constant element, open to static and limiting definition. It was continually being created, constantly evolving as a result of the life we led.

Foucault was to absorb many ideas from Hegel, Heidegger and Sartre. Yet equally significant were the ideas he rejected. In an important way he formed himself in reaction to these philosophers, especially Sartre. As a personality and a thinker, Sartre dominated the Parisian intellectual scene and would remain a constant presence almost throughout Foucault's life: an example and a goad to his aspirations. Sartre's ideas would perform a similar role. Foucault was temperamentally averse to remaining in anyone's shadow for long. He not only had ambition but also sufficient contrariness to strike out on his own – even though his reactive impulse often outran his ideas. There would be no father figures for Foucault; one had been enough.

The young man was maturing at an exceptional rate, both academically and personally. His increasing intellectual assurance was matched by his emotional self-understanding. He was learning to accept his homosexuality, and the violence in his character was subsumed by occasional sado-masochistic role-playing.

By now Foucault's intellectual abilities were beginning to attract the attention of leading figures attached to the ENS, who would discuss their ideas with him. Foucault's former examiner Georges Canguilhem was developing an entirely new structural history of science. In his view, science did not progress by some gradual and inevitable evolution. The history of science involved a number of distinct discontinuities, where knowledge would take an unprecedented step forward into some new realm. (Einstein's relativity is perhaps the best-known example in the last century.) Canguilhem was unusual in having qualifications in both philosophy and medicine. This enabled him to ask, with some acumen, 'What is psychology?' Ironically he attacked psychology on the very ground that it saw as its function and strength: knowledge of self. What was the basis of psychological knowledge? What precisely was it doing, or trying to do? Such questions were of particular interest to Foucault, whose earlier erratic behaviour had brought him into first-hand contact with institutional psychiatry. He had been temperamentally averse to the role of patient, and disillusioned with the psychology behind the treatment offered him. This had prompted him to 'forget the whole thing the moment my shrink went on holiday'. Now here was Canguilhem articulating what he had instinctively felt was wrong with psychology – its lack of self-knowledge about what it was and what it was doing.

Foucault also attracted the attention of Louis Althusser, who was then a young instructor at the ENS. During the war Althusser had survived five years in concentration camps, and as a result had become a convinced Marxist. He was now developing Marxist theory in what would later be seen as a structuralist direction. In reading Marx, he argued, one had to look beyond the surface text. It was necessary to be aware of the 'horizon of thought' that limited Marx's language and concepts to his particular historical period. One had to try to understand the fundamental problems that Marx was actually dealing with (even though he may not always have been aware of them himself). Althusser persuaded Foucault to become a member of the French Communist Party (PCF). Despite its Stalinism, the PCF remained a major political force in France, largely as a result of the heroic role it had played in the Resistance during the Nazi occupation. But Foucault felt ill at ease with the party and attended few meetings. Having come to terms with his sexuality and accepted its centrality in his life, he was not enamoured to hear homosexuality dismissed by the party as mere 'bourgeois decadence'. (Althusser was to remain a leading Marxist influence on students at the ENS for well over thirty years, until he strangled his wife in 1981. As a result, he spent his last decade confined in an asylum, where he wrote a brilliant autobiography in which he confessed how little Marx he had actually read.)

In 1951 Foucault took his final exams, achieving a brilliant result – as usual, on the second try. He was now faced with the prospect of military service. His record of 'depression', however, together with what appears to have been some family string-pulling, ensured that he was excused this waste of two years. He now continued working as an instructor at the ENS, specialising in philosophy and psychology. His interest in the latter led him to become a frequent visitor to the psychiatric unit at the Hôpital Sainte-Anne. Here he soon came to be regarded as virtually an unpaid member of staff, and was even allowed to deal with patients in a clinical capacity. Back at the ENS he became renowned for giving students Rorschach association tests 'so I can know what's on their mind'.

But all this was more than just inkblot tests on good-looking students, and a former patient helping run the asylum. Foucault was now beginning to ask serious questions about psychology, questions that went beyond the promptings of Althusser. How could one study 'experience' scientifically? Human existence was not amenable to objective study: it must be approached by way of its humanity. This could be done by studying the very concept of humanity and how it had evolved.

Foucault now discovered the philosopher who was to transform his entire understanding. Chronologically Nietzsche had preceded and heavily influenced Heidegger; it was as if Foucault was discovering the very roots of his own thinking. Through the long hot August of 1953 Foucault lay on the beach at Civitavecchia (the ancient port of Rome), avidly absorbing the message of the 'philosopher of power'. Nietzsche held up the example of ancient Greece, where the self-destructive forces of Dionysian frenzy achieved both power and beauty when they were contained within the clear, clean discipline of Apollonian form. Both were equally necessary, and this applied to the individual as well as the work of art. The truth about oneself was not 'something given, something which we have to discover – it is something we must create ourselves'. Even humanity itself was simply a social structure, created by changing and contingent cultural forces. This was just the message that Foucault had been waiting to hear. Before reading Nietzsche, he said he had the feeling he 'had been trapped'. Now he understood that he was free to create himself as he saw fit.

But there were wider lessons to be learned here. Just as Foucault had suspected, humanity could be studied only by tracing the history of its development. It was as if his subjective existence and his understanding of humanity itself had suddenly come together. He read: 'Man needs what is most evil in him to achieve what is best in him . . . The secret of harvesting the greatest fruitfulness and the greatest enjoyment from existence is – *to live dangerously*.' Indeed, it was the erotic that drove one to the limits of possibility. Despite such bravado, Nietzsche had almost entirely repressed his own sexuality. But Nietzsche's message was music to a sado-masochist's ears. And from here it was just one step to the larger picture: Nietzsche's stress on the central role of power in all human activity struck Foucault like a thunderbolt. This was how the world worked!

Life wasn't all philosophy, of course. Foucault was, after all, living in Paris. The up-and-coming young psychologist-cum-philosopher had now begun to socialise in the intellectual cafés of the Left Bank. One night he struck up a conversation with a young composer named Jean Barraqué. Foucault enjoyed contemporary classical music, without fully comprehending its technical complexities. Yet he soon decided that Barraqué was 'one of the most brilliant and underrated composers of the present generation'. (Besides being a classic example of psychological self-displacement, this also turned out to be a unique judgement of great foresight, to be confirmed only after both men were dead.)

Barraqué was two years younger than Foucault, an intense, highly strung artist who wore glasses to counteract his frowning shortsightedness. He drank heavily, but his powerful modernist music was suffused with clarity and formal precision. He too was a fervent admirer of Nietzsche. Foucault and Barraqué were instantly attracted to each other and were soon passionately in love. Intense philosophical discussion, alcoholic abandon, sado-masochistic sex – such were the intoxicating ingredients of their frenzied affair. Foucault was utterly absorbed; Barraqué both gave, and possessively demanded, everything. For Foucault, his life had invaded his thought, and his thought had invaded his life. For both men, music and philosophy became one. Barraqué's *Séquence*, which contains a Nietzschean text suggested by Foucault, has the lines: 'Must we not hate ourselves if we are to love ourselves . . . *I am your labyrinth*.' The sexuality that was sublimated in Nietzsche was lived by Barraqué and Foucault. At the same time the character of this music was to be uncannily prescient where Foucault's historical and philosophical understanding was concerned. Another piece of Barraqué's music from this period was described as 'a summit of agonising grandeur; the relentless process is coming to an end now, and Music cracks under the inhuman strain, disintegrates and is sucked into the void. Whole slabs of sound crumble and vanish beneath the all-engulfing ocean of silence.' Not only music but history and truth could be like this, Foucault was beginning to realise. And so could love.

But no relationship could last at such a frenzied pitch. Barraqué's possessiveness developed into a paranoid jealousy; Foucault's wayward independence was beginning to feel stifled. And both men were aware that their drinking was getting out of hand. After one particularly volcanic row, they decided that a cooling-off period might be advisable. In August 1955 Foucault accepted a junior post at the University of Uppsala in southern Sweden. Although both men promised otherwise, their relationship would not survive the long separations they now experienced. (Barraqué continued to compose, but never again at such a pitch. His behaviour became increasingly erratic, and he died in 1973 of alcoholism.)

In Sweden, Foucault found a certain peace. It was as if he had weathered a storm. He now emerged a somewhat more mature human being, more at ease with himself – though there was no mistaking the burning ambition that still drove this more relaxed thirty-year-old. He bought himself a flashy Jaguar (supposedly for the thousand-mile journeys back to Paris each vacation). His hair began to thin, and he took to wearing an eye-jarring tartan suit. During the long winters he became a popular dinner-party host. His skilled French cooking was a revelation, and the profusion of wine often produced a similar effect. When lonely he cruised for men in his Jag. Everything was allowed in Sweden, yet eventually the blandness of it all began to pall. As he later remarked, sometimes freedom can become as repressive as direct repression.

Foucault lectured on French literature to classes of mainly female students. Characteristically he chose a rather restricted aspect of this subject, entitling his course, 'The Conception of Love in French Literature from the Marquis de Sade to Jean Genet.' What his audience of healthy eighteen-year-old Swedish girls made of this catalogue of sadism, sodomy and profligate degeneracy is difficult to imagine. Meanwhile Foucault worked long hours researching further psychological and medical oddities for his doctoral thesis. Alas, this proved a bit much even for the tolerant Swedish authorities, who rejected it with the euphemism that it was 'too literary'.

But Foucault was following his instincts. The potent mix of Nietzschean philosophy, psychology, history and clinical practice was leading him into new territory which transgressed the usual academic boundaries. By the time he returned to Paris at the age of thirty-three, Foucault had concentrated his interests on one all-embracing subject. He began writing his 'History of Madness' (later published as *Madness and Civilisation*). This had an ambitious agenda. His intention was not to record a clearer picture of what had taken place in the past. Precisely the opposite: the clearer picture would be of the present. (He would describe his history as 'counter-memory'.) He sought to show how the very concept of madness itself had changed through the ages, and what this meant. The attitude towards madness was in fact a matter of social perception and practice. Foucault wished to uncover the 'zero point' where madness became separated from reason. At what point had madness first been confined, and thus cut off from reason, so that it became 'un-reason'?

In mediaeval times the mad had wandered free in society. They were considered holy. According to Foucault's analysis, the humanism and learning of the Renaissance introduced a subtle change in this attitude. The holiness of madness was transformed into the more humanist concept of 'wisdom'. The wise fool was an ironic reflection of the folly of society. Shakespeare's fools spoke the truth in oblique fashion. Don Quixote's madness reflected the folly of humanity.

The Renaissance was followed by the Classical Age (known more pertinently in the English-speaking world as the Age of Reason). This age may be said to have begun with Descartes, the founder of modern philosophy. Descartes famously used reason to doubt everything, so that he could arrive at some bedrock of truth. How can I know anything for certain? What if my senses are deceiving me? What if the world is a dream, or a mere hallucination? Some 'evil genius' may even be deceiving me concerning the truths of mathematics. No, all I know for certain is that I am thinking. *Cogito ergo sum* ('I think therefore I am'). Indicatively, Foucault noted, Descartes' thoroughgoing doubt did not go so far as to question his own sanity. Reason now reigned supreme – and unquestioned. (Ironically, there was no *reason* for this – which is why reason's supremacy was contingent, not in any way necessary, logical or inevitable.) Reason now became the guiding principle of all intellectual thought, and in doing so became separated from unreason. Such thinking was soon reflected in practice. Within six years of Descartes' death the Hôpital Général was founded in Paris for the confinement of the mad, along with other indigents, beggars and criminals. It was said that one in a hundred Parisians was now locked up.

Madness had become unreason and was now physically separated from the realm of reason. And along with madness, other kinds of 'unreasonable' behaviour were also separated from 'reasonable' society. Soon beggars and the idle were joined by the likes of homosexuals, vagrants and public drunkards. No longer did the fool speak wisdom – he was silenced and banished from public life. Worse still, he was soon reduced to an object of ridicule or a moral warning. Visiting asylums to view the incarcerated and whipped inmates in their cowed or raving degradation became a popular entertainment. No fewer than 96,000 people each year would visit the Bethlehem Hospital for the insane in London. (The corruption of this name gave us the word *bedlam*. Appropriately, the building that was once the original bedlam now houses the Imperial War Museum.) This 'discontinuity' between the Renaissance and the Classical Age saw madness reduced to a scandal, a crime. As madness became defined (and confined), so did reasonable behaviour. Rational speculation about society came up with such notions as the work ethic and moral obligations, which became incorporated in civil law. Deviancy became unreason. This new knowledge thus became a new power, with an intimate connection between the two.

According to Foucault, there then followed a further discontinuity. By the end of the Classical Age reformers came to see this confinement of the mad as barbaric. Madness was not a criminal matter, it was an illness and should be treated as such. Now the insane were liberated from incarceration and placed under medical care. But as the body was freed, the mind became captive. Instead of chains, medication became the order of the day. By the end of the nineteenth century Freud had taken this one stage further. Madness was no longer silenced, it was encouraged to talk on the psychiatrist's couch. But this freedom also contained its own further confinement. A psychiatric discourse was established, together with a structure that subjected the patient to the all-powerful, all-knowing psychiatrist. In all this process Foucault saw a mirror of authoritarian bourgeois society.

Madness was now defined (and confined) by psychiatry. Reason became psychological health. As we can see, here the very word *reason* begins to shift in meaning – so as to align itself with the different definition of madness. By showing how the concept of madness had changed and altered its limits through the ages, Foucault sought to free the present from its own limited vision. The only way for madness to elude this all-powerful authority of reason was for it to live in itself. But how? This could only be achieved by certain artists and philosophers whose extremes and excesses reached beyond the confines of reason. Foucault cites Van Gogh, de Sade and Artaud in this context. With less justification he also mentions Nietzsche, who was in fact silenced by his insanity. Although Foucault is correct with regard to Nietzsche's attitude: 'No man without chaos in him can give birth to a dancing star.' These artists and philosophers express madness 'in itself', and in doing so turn the tables. Confronted with their works, the world of reason is forced to justify itself! Such art and imagination distorts and extends our accepted perception of reason. (Here Van Gogh's *Starry Night* speaks for itself.)

It is no coincidence that around this period the Scottish psychiatrist R.D. Laing was making important practical discoveries about the nature of madness. According to Laing, the apparently incomprehensible and self-contradictory language of the schizophrenic is often a gnomic expression of the twisted truth that the patient is unable to express. Schizophrenia is frequently induced by the self-contradictory situation in which the patient finds himself. (As, for instance, with two quarrelling parents who bequeath their bewildered offspring a divided – i.e., schizoid – reality.)

In his *Madness and Civilisation*, Foucault demonstrated how our idea of madness had undergone discontinuities that were essentially contingent. That is, such changes were in no way logical or necessary. They themselves were unreasonable! These changes of knowledge were also accompanied by significant shifts of power (freedom, incarceration, treatment). This, Foucault suggests, is no isolated case. The emergence of any knowledge system is always linked with a shift in power. Psychology and the role of the patient are just one example. Economics, sociology, even science: the emergence and the development of such knowledge systems is always accompanied by significant shifts in power.

When *Madness and Civilisation* was published in 1961 it established Foucault as a leading intellectual figure in Paris. The fiercely competitive market of French intellectual fashion was undergoing sweeping change. The old guard was becoming old hat. Sartre and existentialism, structuralism, and the endless fluctuations of the latest Marxism were being superseded. Derrida and deconstructionism, Barthes and semiotics, and now Foucault were all coming into fashion. Foucault knew both Derrida and Barthes well: the Left Bank was a small place with a well-known round of intellectual cafés. But under the surface, Foucault's relationship with his new peers would always remain uneasy. Although Foucault's thought had certain limited resemblances to that of Derrida and Barthes, its differences would soon become glaringly apparent.

By now Foucault's father had died. With his inheritance the up-and-coming thirty-four-year-old philosopher bought a flat with a classic view over the *quais* of the Seine on Rue Dr Finlay (named after the nineteenth-century Cuban physician of Scottish-French descent who discovered that the mosquito is the bearer of malaria).

Around this time Foucault met a philosophy student named Daniel Defert, who was a left-wing political activist. France had embarked on a vicious colonial war in Algeria, which both Foucault and Defert opposed. But they differed in their theoretical politics. Foucault refused to concur with Defert's youthful extremist rhetoric: his accusations that de Gaulle's government was running a 'fascist state'. Defert was gay, darkly attractive and ten years younger than Foucault. But what seems to have attracted Foucault most was Defert's passionate political activism. The two soon became lovers; but this was not to be just another casual affair for either of them. Defert eventually moved into Foucault's apartment. They were to remain partners for almost twenty-five years, establishing a deeply affectionate bond. This was strong enough to survive the intermittent tantrums and sulks brought on by the fact that they both insisted upon maintaining an open relationship, occasionally taking other partners. According to Defert, Foucault was extremely easy to live with on a day-to-day basis, and each supported the other in the face of the inevitable prejudice. For all its self-cultivated reputation as a nation of lovers, France remained a Catholic country where homophobia reigned, particularly in academic circles.

In 1963 Foucault published *The Birth of the Clinic: An Archaeology of Medical Perception*. This work is an example of Foucault's immense industry in research: many long hours, day after day, practising his 'archaeology' on original documents in the Bibliothéque Nationale. (Foucault claimed, with only slight exaggeration, that he had read every single book on clinical medicine published between 1790 and 1820.) In this work he shows how at the start of the nineteenth century another discontinuity took place. Classical medicine gave way to clinical medicine. Previously the aim had been to eliminate disease and bring about the health. Now the sick body itself became the focus of medical perception, and the aim of medicine shifted significantly. The vague, apparently self-evident notion of 'health' was replaced with the aim of bringing the patient 'back to "normal" '. (This concept recurs in such descriptions as 'normal temperature', 'normal pulse rate', and so forth.) With the birth of the clinic, medicine became a science, and in doing so became linked to other growing sciences such as anatomy, physiology, chemistry and biology. Taking its place in institutional society brought medicine into relation with political and social structures. The idea of 'normality' (as opposed to health) inevitably, insidiously took on political and social overtones. Here Foucault intends a parallel with his *Madness and Civilisation*, where madness (another opposite of the scientifically defined, socially acceptable 'normality') is isolated in the asylum. Similarly, in medicine the clinic emerges. Once again Foucault traces the shifts of power that take place with the shift of knowledge.

Foucault had not only filled another gap in our social self-knowledge but had linked his history to the dynamic evolution of society itself. He had perceptively noted that so-called history was as full of such holes as a Gruyère cheese. Indeed, it seemed that the history of everything that brought life and colour to human existence remained missing. The history of such subjects as love, greed, cruelty, punishment and the like was completely lacking. How could we hope to understand the shifts in power and structure of society without having explored many of its most salient aspects?

During 1964–1965 Foucault completed the major work that would bring his ideas to prominence throughout the Western world. The aim of *The Order of Things: An Archaeology of the Human Sciences* was no less than to investigate how the concept of humanity itself had evolved and become an object of our knowledge.

First it is necessary to define the terms that had now become central to Foucault's method of investigation. When he talks of 'archaeology' he means the unearthing of the hidden structure of knowledge that pertains to a particular historical period. This consists of the often unconscious assumptions and prejudices (literally prejudgements) that objectively organise and limit the thought of any age. Such things are essentially distinct from subjective bias or even collective ignorance: rather, they are the cast of mind that affects all individual thinkers of that age. For instance, as long as it was assumed that the earth was the centre of the universe, it was impossible even to conceive of the elliptical orbits of the planets. Likewise, as Foucault had shown, without a concept of reason there could be no concept of 'unreason'.

The set of assumptions, prejudices and mind-sets that structured and limited the thought of any particular age was referred to by Foucault as an *episteme*. This word derives from the same ancient Greek root as the branch of philosophy known as epistemology – the investigation of the grounds upon which we base our knowledge. (For instance, consistency. We base our knowledge on the assumption that the physical world behaves in a consistent manner. A certain cause will always give rise to a certain effect. If it doesn't, we automatically assume that the initial cause has somehow altered. This assumption of consistency can never be knowledge but is nonetheless one of the philosophical assumptions on which knowledge is based.) Foucault's episteme is the entire structure of such assumptions: the particular mind-set of a historical period. The episteme marks out the limits of the period's experience, the extent of its knowledge, and even its notion of truth. A particular episteme is bound to give rise to a particular form of knowledge. Foucault called the latter a *discourse*, by which he meant the accumulation of concepts, practices, statements and beliefs that were produced by a particular episteme.

Foucault illustrates the 'historical a priori' nature of the episteme in his introduction to *The Order of Things*. Here he cites the ancient Chinese encyclopedia described in a short story by the Argentinian writer Jorge Luis Borges. This encyclopedia divides all known animals according to an unusual classification: they are listed under such categories as 'those that belong to the Emperor', 'tame animals', 'embalmed animals', and so forth. Such categories may appear bizarre to us, but they make us aware that our own system of categorisation is no more necessarily logical. It is equally contingent: an order we have imposed in line with our particular cultural assumptions (episteme). We consider the species and biological relationships of animals to be more important than who owns them. (We might think differently if the punishment for touching an animal owned by the emperor was castration, as was the case in ancient China.) Borges' story makes us aware that any system of classification will always have its limitations. So what are the limitations of our episteme? we are bound to ask ourselves.

Foucault goes on to explore this question by conducting an 'archaeology' of human sciences. He begins with the Renaissance episteme. Unfortunately he chooses to character-ise this in a particularly blinkered and biased fashion. In Foucault's view, the Renaissance episteme was based upon resemblances: 'similitudes' and correspondences. He illus-trates this by describing the 'doctrine of signatures', which was indeed typical of the Renaissance way of thinking. According to this doctrine, God indicated affinities between things by means of resemblances (or signatures). For instance, an orchid bore an uncanny resemblance to a testicle. This indicated that it could be used in the cure of venereal diseases. Likewise the yellow flower celandine was good for jaundice. For the Renaissance thinker, the world was a book, to be 'read'. Interpretation and metaphorical significance, not observation and scientific experiment, were the order of the day.

This was certainly the case in such sciences as medicine and emergent chemistry (which remained virtually indistinguishable from alchemy). But it was definitely not true of astronomy and biology (given new impetus by the discovery of the telescope and the microscope), anatomy or physics. Foucault cites the work of several Renaissance thinkers, such as the medical pioneer Paracelsus, the mathematician Cardano, and the philosopher Campanella. But besides being a supreme physician, Paracelsus was also an alchemist; likewise Cardano was also an astrologer, and Campanella a utopian. The greatest, and for us most characteristic figures of the Renaissance, are ignored. No mention is made of Copernicus, Galileo or Harvey (whose discovery of the circulation of the blood helped put an end to such old wives' tales as the doctrine of signatures).

Foucault's indication of epistemes was indeed important, but his case was not helped by oversimplification. There was more than one episteme present in Renaissance thought. Or indeed in the thought of one Renaissance man: Copernicus may have discovered the solar system, but he appealed to the authority of the alchemist Hermes Trismegistus in support of his argument. The transformation from one episteme to another was somewhat more complex than Foucault was willing to admit.

Even so, his central point seems undeniable. The Renaissance episteme gave way to the Classical episteme (for us, the episteme of the Age of Reason). Instead of resemblance, thought now turned to distinction. Analysis gave rise to measurement and experiment. The use of reason led to discrimination. Chemical substances were seen to consist of elements or combinations of elements; animals and plants became classified as species; gold was for the first time taken as the ultimate measure of a nation's wealth.

Knowledge was no longer an occult matter, only for the initiated. It was a result of scientific observation, open to all. Yet this episteme based on reason and observation had a curious side effect. In its scientific attempt to clarify the picture, it eliminated the effect of the subject (the observer). The Classical episteme rendered the subject invisible. There was no place for humanity itself as an object of scientific study.

With the advent of the nineteenth century this too would change. Humanity began to be studied as a historical subject. Thinkers as disparate as Darwin, Hegel and Marx now saw humanity as evolving through historical development. Such thinking continued into the twentieth century. The effects of this episteme remained central to Sartre's existentialism, which insisted on 'existence before essence'. In other words, we create our essential selves through our existence; we do not have a given essence. In biology, humanity became the object of anthropological research. In economics, wealth came to be measured in terms of labour rather than inanimate gold. The man of reason acquired depth and became the object of psychology. But, said Foucault, such a state of affairs will not last: 'Before the end of the eighteenth century man did not exist. As the archaeology of our thought easily shows, man is an invention of a recent date. And one perhaps nearing its end.'

Once again Foucault was of course oversimplifying. His research, which limited itself to contemporary documents, was frequently uneven. Brilliant insight was inserted into a patchy overall picture. The individual points he made were illustrative but frequently unsustainable in the general case. It is simply not true that the concept 'man' (or humanity) did not exist as an object of study, speculation and thought before the end of the eighteenth century. Examples abound: from mortal questionings prompted by divine awe in the Bible, to Plato's vain attempt at a logical definition of humanity (the famous 'featherless biped', which prompted one of Plato's more irreverent students to sling a plucked chicken over the wall into the Academy). And Shakespeare is of course filled with such speculations, from Hamlet's troubled ponderings to:

> But man, proud man
> Dress'd in a little brief authority,
> Most ignorant of what he's most assur'd,
> His glassy essence, like an angry ape . . .

Foucault would have argued that these were not part of the archaeology of the human sciences. But there will always be occasions when psychological insight extends beyond literature into science and philosophy.

Yet Foucault's point that the 'recently invented' concept of humanity may be nearing its end has considerable force. As our knowledge of DNA expands, and our expertise in genetic manipulation increases, the concept of humanity may well become redundant. Drastic transformation lies some way in the future. But progressive alterations (especially of 'defective' genes) will certainly begin to erode our idea of what precisely a human being is, and what it means to be human.

At the same time Foucault began promoting the idea of the episteme, on the other side of the Atlantic the American historian of science Thomas S. Kuhn came up with the remarkably similar idea of the paradigm. Foucault's epistemes were discovered by archaeology in the wide cultural field of the human sciences. Kuhn's paradigms applied more exclusively and particularly to science itself. 'Paradigm shifts' accounted for the big, spectacular advances in science – such as those provided by Copernicus, Newton or Einstein. After such advances, our vision of the world could never be the same again. Each of these thinkers discovered an innovative way of thinking which provided a model for future research. After Einstein, time and space (and matter and energy) could no longer be seen as absolutes: they were relative.

But such thinking was to rebound in an unexpected way. The trouble with both Foucault and Kuhn was that they appeared to destroy any absolute notion of truth. If our way of thinking was always blinkered by an episteme (or paradigm), it appeared we could never arrive at the 'truth'. Likewise, if all epistemes were contingent, how could we prove that one episteme was better than another? We couldn't. So all truth was relative; it just depended upon how you looked at things. Such simplistic criticisms do little damage to either Foucault or Kuhn. The point is that one episteme (or paradigm) will prove more useful (or theoretically fruitful) than another. It will provide a closer approximation to the ever-unattainable perfect picture (i.e., 'absolute truth') of what actually happens. *Something* undeniably happens, but our perceptual apparatus enables us to experience only certain effects of these events. The belief in our ability to discover absolute truth entails the belief that our perceptual apparatus – and its extension in scientific instruments – is an absolute match for the actuality of what happens. Our eyes register light only between ultraviolet and infrared. How can we know that our scientific instruments, which only extend our perceptual field, are not similarly limited? And in what way can our visual experience of 'red' be said to be an absolute match for electromagnetic radiation with a wavelength of 7×10^{-15} cms? But surely $2 + 2 = 4$ is an absolute truth? Perhaps; but as Einstein pointed out, 'As far as the laws of mathematics refer to reality, they are not certain, and as far as they are certain, they do not refer to reality.' It is within this gap that the paradigms of Kuhn operate. Likewise Foucault's epistemes – though these tend to apply to the wider, less precise cultural realm.

In 1964 Foucault's partner Defert was called up for military service and chose volunteer work rather than the army. He was sent to teach in Tunisia. Rather than face a long separation, Foucault eventually followed him, accepting a post as visiting professor at the University of Tunis. Here he soon settled into an agreeable Mediterranean style of life, taking up residence in a designer-converted stable in the French artists' colony at Sidi-Bou-Said. In Tunis, Foucault was able to enjoy the best of both worlds, French and North African cuisine, wine and cannabis, intellectual debate in the cafés, and good-looking young Arabs. At the university he lectured on Nietzsche and elaborated on the cultural insights from his research into the modern episteme.

Some critics had now begun to regard Foucault as 'the new Kant'. They compared his concept of the episteme to the notion of the 'synthetic a priori' developed by Kant at the end of the eighteenth century. Put simply, Kant had insisted that we cannot help but see the world as if through 'space-time' spectacles. Foucault's description of the inevitably limited and structured thought associated with an episteme did appear to be a development of this idea. But to compare Foucault's ensuing cultural insights with the cathedral-like grandeur of Kant's philosophical system was plainly ludicrous. Even Foucault, initially flattered, soon began to grow tired of such hyperbole.

But Foucault's comfortable life as a philosophical celebrity in exile (with *Le Monde* flown in every morning) was soon shattered. In December 1966 the students of Tunis demonstrated against the increasingly repressive regime of President Habib Bourguiba. Encouraged by Defert, Foucault actively sided with the students. For the first time in his life he now became 'fully politicised', in the view of his partner. On one occasion Foucault was beaten by the police, and afterwards he sheltered fugitive students in his flat.

But his stay in Tunis meant that Foucault missed out on the greatest French political event of his adult life: the 1968 *événements* in Paris. During May, Parisian students took over the entire Left Bank, effectively bringing the capital to a standstill. Activists and Left Bank philosophers delivered impromptu speeches to assemblies of cheering students. Even de Gaulle temporarily lost his nerve and fled in secret to a French military base in Germany. It was several weeks before the batons and water cannons of the riot police finally broke through the street barricades and regained control. By chance, Defert was in Paris – but throughout *les événements* he kept his partner informed of the latest developments by phone.

A thousand miles away on another continent, Foucault fretted. Yet his distance from the events in Paris enabled him to think clearly about what was happening. He came to the conclusion that a new kind of politics was emerging, one that could well transform society. From now on Foucault would remain politically active and believe that his philosophy was a political instrument. This was the sixties: everything was being questioned, anything was possible. As Foucault turned towards the youthful activists, they for their part turned towards the latest philosophical approach offered by 'the new Kant'. From now on Foucault would find himself addressing a far wider audience. His work would be translated into all major languages, his books 'liberated' from bookshops everywhere from Berkeley to Buenos Aires.

Later in 1968 Foucault returned to Paris. He had now turned forty and was becoming concerned about his ageing appearance. Irritated by his thinning hair, he decided to shave his head. He also took to wearing a white polo-neck sweater and corduroy suit 'to save ironing'. The image of the bald, bespectacled, 'chic-tough' philosopher was created. Now there was an unmistakeable public face to front the words: the legend of Foucault was born.

In Paris, Foucault took up an appointment at the trendy experimental University of Vincennes, which had been set up on the eastern outskirts of the city. He was officially designated 'chairman' of the philosophy department. (Professors were out, Chairman Mao was in.)

The French education system had long been overdue for reform. Things were so regimented it was said that at eleven o'clock on any given morning the minister of education knew precisely which page of which textbook was being studied in every classroom throughout France. The University of Vincennes was determined to lead the way forward into a brave new educational world. Instead of being run by rigid fiat (as Foucault's father had run his hospital medical school), the university was to operate by 'participation'. Foucault quickly managed to get Defert appointed to the sociology department just in time for the first student riots. The university now became a battlefield between Maoists, student activists, Communists, Marxists and the latest splinter groups of all these factions, who converged on the campus from all over Paris. (The metro route out from the Left Bank even became known as the 'party line'.)

Still the sad victims of their misguided education, the police had no alternative but to act in the way they had been taught. Enthusiastically they stormed the school with tear gas and truncheons to break up the demonstrators, and this time Foucault was able to mount the barricades in his stylish corduroy suit. Alas, his familiar bald head and white polo-neck sweater made him an instant target, and he was lucky to get away with only a vicious going-over from the *flics*.

But Foucault now had his admirers in high places. He was seen by some as the rising French intellectual star who would replace the ageing Sartre on the international scene. Foucault was proposed for election to the hallowed Collège de France, which had been founded in the sixteenth century. This unique institution consisted of fifty leading professors, ranging through all fields from physics to music. The college gave no degrees, but in return for their tenure the professors were required to deliver a course of lectures on their own original work. These lectures were open to the general public, and would attract the sharpest minds in the field. After some persistent lobbying, Foucault was appointed to a newly created chair. As one influential faculty member put it, the college was 'mindful not to let genius slip through [its] fingers'. Owing to the exceptional nature of his field, Foucault was allowed to designate his own title, and became 'professor of the history of systems of thought'.

Foucault's lectures at the Collège de France, and his writing during this period, returned to the Nietzschean basis of his thought. In *The Genealogy of Morals*, Nietzsche had traced the lineage of modern ethical concepts to their origins. For instance, he had shown how much Christianity owed to its early years as the slave religion of the late Roman Empire. (The emphasis on humility, compassion, turning the other cheek: these were how the powerless survived.)

Following on from Nietzsche, Foucault introduced his 'genealogical method'. This sought the 'history of the present' in the development of a wide range of different disciplines or 'knowledges', from literature to medicine. Instead of epistemes, he now laid stress on the 'discourse' of each knowledge. This was the will to truth, but it tended to reject what it did not understand. Why? Because what it did not understand was literally 'useless'. Knowledge was always purposive: it was characterised by a will to dominate or appropriate. It was not some neutral abstract entity. Knowledge was sought for its use; it was potent and unstable. This led Foucault to the concept 'power/knowledge', showing how the two were inextricably linked. Thus the will to truth was only a disguised version of Nietzsche's central will to power, the prime human drive. Foucault's 'genealogy' sought to analyse the relationship between power and any particular 'knowledge'.

But Foucault differed from Nietzsche in one important aspect. For him, power did not so much reside in individuals, such as Nietzsche's notorious 'supermen'. Foucault recognised that the most important aspect of power lay in social relations. Individuals might have power in the form of domination and constraint; but more important, power was also involved in the production and use of knowledge. Amidst the complexity of modern society, with its multitude of checks and balances, this appears a more penetrating analysis.

The shifts and negotiations of power create the spaces where discourses can appear. These knowledges, and indeed all theories, are contingent. So also is the delineation of truth and falsehood within these knowledges. This evolves, grows, undergoes sudden shifts – it has its own genealogy. And because this delineation is contingent, so is the criterion of truth within that particular knowledge.

Once again the notion of absolute truth is fatally undermined. But the relativity of such truths still remains subject to the proviso mentioned earlier. Each different truth is the truth about an actuality as it was conceived at that particular moment. This truth may contain flaws, gaps and even contradictions, but as long as it works well enough for the knowledge to which it applies, it will remain accepted. In other words, so long as it fulfils its *power* requirement.

Examples of this abound in history – from the Ptolemaic picture of the heavens which lasted more than a thousand years, to the even longer history of alchemy. Such a concept of truth is even detectable in the most advanced contemporary 'hard' science. The discrepancy between quantum physics (which is largely applied at subatomic levels) and classical mechanics (which we continue to apply at the everyday level, even in complex engineering) is evident to all scientists. But the 'truth' of both systems is applied, even though it is undeniably contradictory, because both have the *power* to produce *knowledge*, which can then be put to *powerful* use. Neither the quantum nor the classical version of the truth is absolute, and their coexistence is certainly not logical. Even the very latest science is in this way contingent.

Such relativism is in the end acceptable. (There is no alternative.) But Foucault went still further in deconstructing reality. Just as 'truth' is a construct of its discourse, a product of the knowledge in which it applies, so other constructs crop up in the most unlikely places. For instance, in the concept of the 'author' of a work of literature. This concept is not to be identified with an individual human being who sits down at a desk and writes a book. No, says Foucault, the author who produces this work is in fact a construct made from the conjunction of a host of factors, including language, the conception of literature at that particular time in that particular place, and a variety of other social and historical elements. When these are analysed, the notion of the 'author' simply falls apart and vanishes: 'He is not in fact the cause, origin or starting point of the phenomenon of the written or spoken articulation of a sentence; nor is it that meaningful intention which, silently anticipating words, orders them like the visible body of its intuition.' Indeed, the author can 'alter with each sentence'.

This is either self-evident or daft. Any author is of course subject to the influences of his or her circumstances, culture and language. T'would indeed be the utmost in perversitie for this junior scribe to clothe his nakedness i'the stylish apparel of a senior age. Likewise, as demonstrated, an author can vary from sentence to sentence. But that doesn't mean I've vanished in a puff of smoke. Foucault's idea that the author is purely the product of his material and circumstances does of course apply as much to himself as to any other author. So the idea of a nonexistent author must presumably have come from a nonexistent author. Either this reflects nothing about his nothingness, or something about his somethingness, so to speak.

Here Foucault has taken his insight to an unwarranted extreme – which was, ironically, very much a product of its era. Foucault's deconstructionism echoes the behaviourist philosophy that was all the rage in the sixties and seventies. According to behaviourism, there is no such thing as 'mind'; all we have are the observable causes of observable effects, in other words behaviour. The resemblance to Foucault's ideas is obvious – though Foucault himself certainly didn't subscribe to behaviourism. Whether this is an argument for or against Foucault's nonexistent subject is left to the interpretation of the reader (who might be interested to know that according to Foucault's analysis, he or she also doesn't exist, except as a cultural construct).

Many of these ideas appeared in Foucault's *The Archaeology of Knowledge*, published in 1969. The book was greeted with widespread acclaim abroad and lengthy vitriolic demolition in Parisian intellectual circles (a sure sign that one has entered the pantheon of French culture). Foucault and Defert moved into a pristine modern apartment high on the Rue de Vaugirard, one of the Left Bank's main thoroughfares. The eighth-floor view allowed Foucault to pursue a new hobby: voyeurism of young men in the apartments across the street (aided by his powerful binoculars). The skylight enabled him to take up an old one: growing cannabis as he had done in Tunis. And in the evenings he entertained fashionable guests, such as Julie Christie and Jean Genet, with his culinary expertise. But there was also a darker side which few but his closest friends saw. More and more frequently the fashionable intellectual in his white polo neck and corduroys would become transformed into the exotic leather-clad creature of the night who cruised the SM bars. Those who encountered him in this guise speak of the experience as eerie.

In 1970 Foucault was invited to lecture in Tokyo, and in the same year he gave a highly acclaimed course of lectures at the University of California in Berkeley. In San Francisco he discovered the joys of the bathhouses – cavernous, steamy infernos where literally hundreds of men would gather to participate in fist-fucking, golden showers, and other esoteric practices. What in France was forbidden was celebrated in America. Unlike so many French intellectuals, Foucault readily understood and appreciated the American way of life – and not just its wilder shores.

It is easy to condemn Foucault's sexual behaviour. How could a serious philosopher have conducted himself like this? What would Plato or Spinoza have said? But few of us live as we would like to appear. Shame (and/or hypocrisy) is a seemingly inevitable subtlety of civilised social existence. The more we know about thinkers, especially modern ones, the more strange much of their behaviour appears. Reading between the lines, we can surmise that both the otherworldly Plato and the saintly Spinoza were homosexual. Who is to say what this involved? Such knowledge should promote understanding rather than prejudice. For as Nietzsche put it, 'The degree and kind of a man's sexuality reach up into the ultimate pinnacle of his spirit.' It is surely no coincidence that the Wittgenstein who famously pronounced, 'Of that which we cannot speak, we must remain silent', was at the same time a secretive homosexual.

Foucault was also becoming more politically active. In 1970 Defert had become a member of the banned revolutionary Maoist group Gauche Prolétarienne (Proletarian Left), a number of whose members were in prison. As a result, Foucault set up the Groupe d'information sur les prisons (Prison Information Group) with the aim of drawing to public attention the inhuman conditions that prevailed in the French penal system. (The execrable Devil's Island off French Guiana, the tropical hellhole featured in the film *Papillon*, had only been closed down just over a decade previously.) Foucault's intentions were both political and humanitarian – together with the inevitable element of self-publicity so necessary to French intellectuals. But he also had a philosophical purpose which was very much an extension of his previous thinking. According to this agenda, the intellectual 'discovers and identifies the weak points, the openings, the lines of force [to be found in] the inertias and constraints of the present situation'. He has no idea of the future, for he 'doesn't know precisely in which direction he is heading or what he will be thinking tomorrow'. Foucault's stated aim, both politically and philosophically, was the 'wish only to make known the reality'.

In the winter of 1972 Foucault lectured at the State University of New York at Buffalo. The frigid eastern winter in desolate upstate New York was all very different from the balmy Californian dream. There may have been less to enthuse about in the eastern United States, but it nonetheless had lessons for the philosopher of power. What he saw was 'gigantic, technological, a little terrifying, that Piranesi aspect which permeates the view that many Europeans have of New York'. He arranged to visit Attica State Prison, which had recently been the scene of bloody riots. Here he found very different circumstances from the naked brutality, squalor and degradation of the French penal system. It was as if he had stepped into a new historical episteme. 'What struck me perhaps first of all was the entrance, like a phoney Disneyland fortress with observation posts disguised as mediaeval turrets. And behind this ridiculous façade which dwarfs everything else, you discover that the place is nothing more than an immense machine for elimination . . . a sort of prodigious stomach . . . which ingests, consumes, breaks down and then excretes . . . which consumes in order to elimate further what has already been eliminated from society.'

Sado-masochism, the penal system, the philosophy of power – in Foucault's next book the personal and the public, both in his thought and in his life, would merge in a single work. This was *Discipline and Punish: The Birth of the Prison*. Despite its title the book was not limited solely to prisons but also covered institutions such as schools, factories and even hospitals. Foucault recognised that in such places power did not merely oppress, it also affected the oppressor. All those who worked within such systems were linked by a complex web of power relations. Ever wishing to keep abreast of the latest developments in science, Foucault christened his subject 'the microphysics of power'.

But this was to be no abstract examination of minute subtleties. On the opening page Foucault quotes a contemporary document relating to an eighteenth-century execution – one guaranteed to set the pulse racing of even the most latent sado-masochist. The fanatic Robert Damiens had failed to assassinate Louis XV at Versailles, and on 2 March 1757 was required to make 'honourable amends' in front of the Church of Paris. This seemingly innocuous sentence involved the prisoner in the following quaint ceremony: 'on a scaffold the flesh will be torn from his breasts, arms, thighs and calves with red-hot pincers, his right hand, holding the knife with which he committed the said parricide, burnt with sulphur, and, on those places where the flesh will be torn away, poured molten lead, boiling oil, burning resin, wax and sulphur melted together, and then his body drawn and quartered by four horses and his limbs and body consumed by fire . . .' and so on. Foucault's quoted description of these events continues over the first four pages of the book. It includes reference to the 'horrible . . . profuse cries' of the victim, and lingers over how the executioner, whose name was Samson, found it 'so difficult to tear away the pieces of flesh that he set about the same spot two or three times, twisting the pincers as he did so'. Foucault then quotes at instructive length the debacle of the quartering process, when the four whipped horses tied to the prisoner's limbs proved insufficient to pull him apart, then six were not enough, and finally the (still conscious) Damiens had to be hacked apart with a knife by Samson.

Philosophy had never been like this. Even Plato's description of Alcibiades' persistent attempts to seduce Socrates paled by comparison – though perhaps Nietzsche's admonition, 'Going to see a woman? Do not forget your whip,' had hinted at the direction philosophy was taking. Yet having grabbed his reader (or worse), did Foucault have anything important to say? He explains that the birth of the prison took place around the turn of the eighteenth century, when torture and public execution gave way to incarceration. Instead of simply destroying the body of the individual criminal, society took control over it. Similar transformations took place throughout society as the body became subjected to power. Drill was introduced in the army; the factories of the Industrial Revolution required a regulated and disciplined workforce. This was the period when Napoleon was laying the foundations of modern France. Such developments involved a more comprehensive control over society: a new judicial system, new regulations, the attempt to organise many aspects of public life. The time-honoured ways of the countryside gave way to a stuctured urban existence.

Foucault examines this process in microcosm with the birth of the prison. The penal institution did not arise because of the philanthropy of reformers and humanitarian changes to criminal law. It was, rather, the natural consequence of the regulatory and disciplined society that was beginning to emerge. The power that had once merely crushed the body was now becoming articulated, taking control over that body. In prisons, as well as in schools, factories and the army, the body was being subjected to discipline and surveillance. Foucault cites the classic example of Jeremy Bentham's 'panopticon' (literally 'see-all') for prisons. In essence this was a domelike structure, with a raised observing platform beneath its midpoint. This enabled one central observer to spy on the cells situated below, around the rim of the dome. Each of the prisoners in these cells was thus aware that his activities could be observed at any moment. Here was the archetypal image of the new society. The parallel with Foucault's previous histories was evident. Incarceration involved control and knowledge. Power and knowledge were one.

Yet inevitably power itself undergoes a transformation here. In Foucault's analysis it is no longer substantive. That is, it no longer has substance in the former manner. It is not absolute and wielded by one central person – as, say, in the absolute monarchy of Louis XV. Power now becomes a 'technology': it is the technique by which a society regulates its members. The modern individual was created amidst this plethora of rules and regulations. In many ways he created himself in reaction to these restraints. This may be seen in the archetypal figure of the dandy. Rather than have his individuality extinguished, the dandy felt the need to express himself – in an extravagant and visible manner which circumvented the increasing number of rules and regulations.

Foucault continues by showing how the birth of the prison was accompanied by the birth of many social sciences, among them criminology, sociology and psychology. The inmates of the penal system could be studied and defined, in just the same way as notions of normality had developed as soon as madness was incarcerated. Society's power over its own 'inmates' was further increased by the development of other new sciences. Economics, history and geography all took on scientific aspects during this period. Knowledge/ power led to further understanding as well as further control.

Foucault's historical arguments are both partial and unscientific. His sketch of historical development may well apply to France, in its transformation from the absolute monarchy of the Bourbons to the post-Napoleonic era. Historical development was significantly different in the United States, Britain and Germany. Yet Foucault has a point: behind these differences there remains a spectral similarity. Once again, however, Foucault's insight seems to have been extended far beyond its limit – into something suspiciously resembling theory. Likewise Foucault's historical exemplars often appear shaky. Bentham's panopticon would seem to resemble the mediaeval idea of an all-seeing God more than the power enforcement of nineteenth-century society.

As usual, Foucault's ideas derived heavily from earlier thinkers. These included the usual suspects, such as Kant, Nietzsche and Heidegger. But this time he also drew from Émile Durkheim, the nineteenth-century French founder of modern sociology. Durkheim had argued against the prevailing British and American idea that the individual, and individual self-interest, formed the basis of society, and that society itself was simply an artificial concept or idea. (This attitude lingers on in Margaret Thatcher's remark, 'There is no such thing as society.') Durkheim stressed the primacy of society over the individual. He emphasised social integration bound by shared moral belief, and sought to identify the sources of social disruption. Foucault's ideas concerning the 'techniques' of power are very much an extension of Durkheim.

Foucault also downgrades the personality – which, like the 'author', is considered a mere construct. His socio-historical analysis therefore suffers from a blind spot with regard to the effect of important historical personalities. This is a curious omission for one who grew up in the shadow of Hitler and Stalin, and spent several years defining his political stance towards de Gaulle. The relevance of Foucault's ideas to American development is even more wayward. The transformations in American life brought about by technology, the mass media, and entrepreneurial capitalism remain largely unaccounted for. In such aspects the American experience is to a large extent the experience of the Western world (even France). It simply cannot be ignored. If Foucault's theory of power does not account for this, it does not account for the twentieth century.

In 1975 Foucault returned to the University of California at Berkeley. Down the road at the University of California at San Diego, the Marxist Herbert Marcuse was excoriating the 'one-dimensional man' of Western society. Everything was being questioned, and California was a ferment of ideas – from the sensational to the plain silly. (While Timothy Leary was urging people to 'Tune in, turn on, drop out,' at Caltech the likes of Richard Feynman and Murray Gell-Mann were solving the fiendish difficulties of quantum electro-dynamics.) Foucault was determined to shine. His lectures theorised about a wide variety of abnormal sex. And between his teaching engagements he embarked upon an industrious programme of research in the bathhouses and SM parlours of San Francisco. He took an acid trip in the desert and was nearly run down attempting to cross a freeway while high on morphine. He justified his behaviour on theoretical grounds. Desire was hampered by 'concepts of naturalistic restriction' and 'physical limit': we had to burst 'beyond desire' into pleasure. In this way pleasure could never be 'abnormal', like desire. Likewise, sado-masochism subverted power (pain) by eroticising it (into pleasure).

Skating on such theoretical thin ice might have had its pitfalls in Paris, but this was California – which was now moving on from the triumphs of sixties behaviour to the theories of the seventies. The flower people had given way to the Black Panthers. Foucault decided to write a history of sexuality in three volumes. These mix sense with nonsense, and a lot of unexpectedly boring sexual history. The first volume claims (without irony) to be 'An Introduction' to sexuality. In this Foucault makes the interesting assertion that following the Renaissance sexuality was 'internalised' by the repressive powers in society. Medicine and psychology now began to exert their power over the body, and thus sexuality became subjected to social control. Such casual generalisations, even backed by a welter of contemporary documentation, indicate the diminishing returns of Foucault's philosophy. They are also inaccurate. During much of the eighteenth century the British, for instance, lived at ease with their sexuality for perhaps the only time between the Elizabethan and the hippie era. (This too is a wicked generalisation. But I don't intend to float a theory on it, merely to torpedo one.)

In the second volume of his history of sexuality Foucault turns to ancient Greece, an era rich in frank eroticism. Unfortunately he uses his explorations of Greek behaviour to explain how sexuality became incorporated within the moral code. But did this really happen in ancient Greece? Sexuality is so central to our evolution that prohibitions are found in the most primitive societies. Even in animals, sexual practice is accompanied by something remarkably similar to embryonic moral behaviour. We must step outside society, if only temporarily, if we wish to elude sexual morality. In this sense the bathhouse and the orgy chamber may be said to offer refuge from the irksome restraints of civilisation. But the only place within society where sexuality has ever been entirely free of moral restraint has been the fantasising adolescent mind. (And in this we are all adolescents.)

The third volume of Foucault's history progresses to ancient Rome. Here, amidst all the 'sexual discourse', Foucault does have some interesting things to say about 'the culture of the self'. He sketches the growth of subjectivity: how it developed into 'an attitude, a way of behaving', and 'permeated ways of living'. Its procedures were 'reflected upon, developed and taught'. In this way subjectivity became 'a social practice giving rise to inter-individual relations'. Such exchanges and communications would on occasion even give rise to social institutions.

In May 1984 Foucault finally delivered the manuscript of the third volume of his history of sexuality to his publisher. Two weeks later, on 2 June, he collapsed and was hospitalised. For two years he had found himself suffering from frequent semidebilitating illnesses. Only now did their import become clear. Foucault had AIDS. The end was sudden; on 25 June Foucault died. His funeral attracted hundreds of mourners. These included celebrities from all sectors of Parisian cultural life, many of whom were deeply moved. Despite prickly intellectual controversies, Foucault was a sympathetic personality, and many regarded him as a close personal friend.

BY AND ABOUT FOUCAULT: SOME QUOTES, CRITICISMS AND IDEAS

More consistently than any other contemporary thinker, Michel Foucault has developed the implications of Nietzsche's rejection of the Platonic idea of truth. In its place he proposes what may be called, in Deleuze's phrase, a 'counter-philosophy' which traces the lowly origins of truth in struggle and conflict, in arbitrariness and contingency, in a will to truth that is essentially intricated with desire and power.

Kenneth Baynes, *After Philosophy*

Some of Foucault's central ideas:

In the Classical Age (Age of Reason) madness became separated from reason and the concept of 'unreason' was born. It was then that madness was confined to the asylum.

An *episteme* is the structure of thought which epitomises the thinking of a particular age. It is the underground network of assumptions and thought processes, the 'mind-set', which limits the scientific, philosophical, and cultural thinking of an age.

Archaeology is the technique of unearthing the rules of thought that limited the concepts of a particular age. Foucault practised this by studying original documents from the period.

Genealogy was the term Nietzsche used to describe his study of moral concepts. This enabled him to trace their evolution: what they originally were, the hidden motives behind them, and how we overlook their origins in our modern attitude towards such concepts. Genealogy traced the history of the will to power.

Foucault used the term to describe his historical analysis of various 'knowledges' – such as literature, medicine and morality. This analysis showed how the notions of 'truth' in these knowledges had altered. Such changes had occurred not in a logical fashion, but were contingent on the episteme of their age. Indeed, our entire conception of truth was contingent.

The 'author' is merely a 'functional principle', which limits the totality of the imagination within the confining 'mind-set' of a particular age.

Foucault claimed that 'the motive that compelled me' was nothing more or less than 'curiosity'. But this was curiosity of a high order: 'The question of knowing if one can think differently than one thinks and perceive differently than one sees is absolutely necessary if one is to go on looking and reflecting at all.'

Foucault at his best:

'The history which bears and determines us has the form of a war rather than that of a language: relations of power, not relations of meaning. History has no "meaning", though that is not to say that it is absurd or incoherent.'

Genealogy seeks to trace the origins of the language we use and the laws by which we are governed. It does this 'in order to reveal the heterogeneous systems which, beneath the mask of our ego, deny us any reality'. Its purpose is 'not to rediscover the roots of our identity, rather to strive to dissipate them'. Genealogy 'attempts to reveal all the discontinuities that traverse us'.

'Each society has its regime of truth, its "general politics" of truth: that is, the types of discourse which it accepts and makes function as true.'

And Foucault at his most ludicrous:

FOUCAULT: 'It's not as simple as that – to enjoy oneself . . . I hope I'll die of an overdose – of pleasure of any kind. Because I think it's really difficult and I always have the feeling that I do not feel *the* pleasure, the complete total pleasure and, for me, it's related to death.'

INTERVIEWER: 'Why would you say that?'

FOUCAULT: 'Because I think that the kind of pleasure I would consider as *the* real pleasure, would be so deep, so intense, so overwhelming that I wouldn't survive it. I would die.'

He goes on to recount that one of the happiest moments of his life was when he was hit by a car (while high on opium). 'I had the impression that I was dying, and it was really a very, very intense pleasure . . . It was, it still is, one of my best memories.'

CHRONOLOGY OF SIGNIFICANT PHILOSOPHICAL DATES

6th C BC	The beginning of Western philosophy with Thales of Miletus.
End of 6th C BC	Death of Pythagoras.
399 BC	Socrates sentenced to death in Athens.
c 387 BC	Plato founds the Academy in Athens, the first university.
335 BC	Aristotle founds the Lyceum in Athens, a rival school to the Academy.
AD 324	Emperor Constantine moves capital of Roman Empire to Byzantium.
AD 400	St Augustine writes his *Confessions*. Philosophy absorbed into Christian theology.
AD 410	Sack of Rome by Visigoths heralds opening of Dark Ages.
AD 529	Closure of Academy in Athens by Emperor Justinian marks end of Hellenic thought.
Mid-13th C	Thomas Aquinas writes his commentaries on Aristotle. Era of Scholasticism.
1453	Fall of Byzantium to Turks, end of Byzantine Empire.

1492	Columbus reaches America. Renaissance in Florence and revival of interest in Greek learning.
1543	Copernicus publishes *On the Revolution of the Celestial Orbs*, proving mathematically that the earth revolves around the sun.
1633	Galileo forced by church to recant heliocentric theory of the universe.
1641	Descartes publishes his *Meditations*, the start of modern philosophy.
1677	Death of Spinoza allows publication of his *Ethics*.
1687	Newton publishes *Principia*, introducing concept of gravity.
1689	Locke publishes *Essay Concerning Human Understanding*. Start of empiricism.
1710	Berkeley publishes *Principles of Human Knowledge*, advancing empiricism to new extremes.
1716	Death of Leibniz.
1739–1740	Hume publishes *Treatise of Human Nature*, taking empiricism to its logical limits.
1781	Kant, awakened from his 'dogmatic slumbers' by Hume, publishes *Critique of Pure Reason*. Great era of German metaphysics begins.
1807	Hegel publishes *The Phenomenology of Mind*, high point of German metaphysics.
1818	Schopenhauer publishes *The World as Will and Representation*, introducing Indian philosophy into German metaphysics.
1889	Nietzsche, having declared 'God is dead', succumbs to madness in Turin.

1921	Wittgenstein publishes *Tractatus Logico-Philosophicus*, claiming the 'final solution' to the problems of philosophy.
1920s	Vienna Circle propounds Logical Positivism.
1927	Heidegger publishes *Being and Time*, heralding split between analytical and Continental philosophy.
1943	Sartre publishes *Being and Nothingness*, advancing Heidegger's thought and instigating existentialism.
1953	Posthumous publication of Wittgenstein's *Philosophical Investigations*. High era of linguistic analysis.

CHRONOLOGY OF FOUCAULT'S LIFE

1926	Paul-Michel Foucault born in Poitiers.
1945	Studies in Paris for second attempt at entry to École Normale Supérieure.
1946–1952	Studies at École Normale Supérieure.
1955–1958	Teaches at University of Uppsala in Sweden.
1960	Meets Daniel Defert, who becomes lifelong companion.
1961	Publishes *Madness and Civilisation*.
1965	Publishes *The Order of Things: An Archaeology of Human Sciences*.
1966–1968	Visiting professor at University of Tunis.
1969	Elected to the Collège de France.
1970	Delivers first lectures in United States.
1972	Lectures at State University of New York at Buffalo. Visits New York State Prison at Attica.
1975	Publishes *Discipline and Punish: The Birth of the Prison*. Lectures at University of California at Berkeley.
1976	Publishes *A History of Sexuality*, Volume 1.
1984	Publishes *A History of Sexuality*, Volume 2.
1984	Dies of AIDS in Paris.
1986	Posthumous publication of *A History of Sexuality*, Volume 3.

RECOMMENDED READING

Michel Foucault, *Madness and Civilisation: A History of Insanity in the Age of Reason* (Random House, 1988). His first major work.

Michel Foucault, *The Order of Things: An Archaeology of the Human Sciences* (Random House, 1994). Contains much of his most penetrating philosophical thinking.

Garry Gutting, ed., *The Cambridge Companion to Foucault* (Cambridge University Press, 1994). Knowledgeable essays covering a wide range of Foucault's thought.

David Macey, *The Lives of Michel Foucault* (Random House, 1995). A full-length biography, integrating the life and thought, and sparing no blushes.

Paul Rabinow, ed., *The Foucault Reader* (Pantheon, 1985). The best available selection from Foucault's works, interviews, etc.

INDEX

A NOTE ON THE AUTHOR

PAUL STRATHERN was educated at Trinity College, Dublin, and lectures in mathematics and philosophy at Kingston University. He has written five novels, one of which won a Somerset Maugham Prize. His most recent works include *Dr Strangelove's Game: A Brief History of Economic Genius* and *Mendeleyev's Dream: The Quest for the Elements*, which was shortlisted for the Aventis Science Prize. He has also written for many journals including the *Observer* (London), *Wall Street Journal* and *New Scientist*. His popular Philosophers in 90 Minutes series is being published worldwide in fifteen languages.